MY GIFT REVEALED MY PURPOSE
Our Gifts Will Make Room for Us

Dr. Onika L. Shirley

Copyright © 2019 Dr. Onika L. Shirley
All rights reserved. No part of this book may be reproduced or transmitted in any form or by any means, electronic or mechanical, including photocopy, recording, or by any information storage and retrieval system with the exception of a reviewer who may quote brief passages in a review to be printed in a blog, newspaper or magazine without written permission from the author. Address inquiries to: unwrappingmygift@gmail.com
Scripture source: New International Version (NIV), Holy Bible, New International Version, NIV copyright 1973,1978,1984, 2011 by Biblica, Inc. unless otherwise noted.

ISBN-13: 978-0-578-50673-9

Printed in the United States of America

DEDICATION

Dr. Onika L. Shirley
I dedicate this book to God Almighty, my creator, my strong tower, my source of inspiration, my wisdom, knowledge, and understanding. God has truly been the source of my strength throughout this book and on His wings only have I soared. My purpose came from God and I thank Him for all my gifts. I also dedicate this book to my children, baby Aubrey grandma's heart, my mother and my sisters and brothers. To God be the glory. We all have a purpose and our gifts will make room for us. We, as a family, were made for greatness so unwrap the gifts God gave you and give them back to the world.

Evangelist John Agbonifo
I dedicate this book to my mom and my centre for help initiative (NGO). The kids who are helpless in Africa and the destitute kids in Edo state Benin City. Life becomes more beautiful when you make people smile... Thanks.

Jo Ann Lipscomb
I give my story to you Jesus because you have made my life your story by giving me Purpose. Thank you! Dr. Onika Shirley, thank you for allowing me to share in the many blessings God is showering down on your life. It's a privileged to be connected to someone who's connected to God. My husband, Paul, you are and will always be my bestie. Thank you for covering me with love and encouraging me to write! My boys, you have always been my world and reason for trying to leave a legacy of "Love for God". Thank you for blessing me with your beautiful family that God has blessed you with. I love you! My sisters, Pam and Donna, thank you for showing me unconditional love, especially when it wasn't easy to do.

CONTENTS

INTRODUCTION ix

MEET THE AUTHORS xiii

Chapter 1: Our Purpose Is to Serve - Dr. Onika Shirley 1

Chapter 2: Embrace Your Life's Purpose - Dr. Onika Shirley 7

Chapter 3: What God Created Me With - Evangelist John Agbonifo 13

Chapter 4: Activating Your Vision - Evangelist John Agbonifo 19

Chapter 5: Discovering Your Purpose – Jo Ann Lipscomb 23

Chapter 6: Living on Purpose - Dr. Onika Shirley 37

Chapter 7: Be Fruitful and Multiply - Evangelist John Agbonifo 45

Chapter 8: You are a Precious Seed - Evangelist John Agbonifo 49

Chapter 9: Purpose Prevails - Jo Ann Lipscomb 57

Chapter 10: Purposed To Take Action, Despite of and Regardless To - Dr. Onika Shirley 69

Conclusion - Dr. Onika Shirley 85

INTRODUCTION

Purpose! We were all created with a purpose. Many people experience the problem of trying to discover their purpose. Has it ever been a problem for you? Has not knowing your purpose ever held you back from moving into areas that could enrich your own life and the lives of others? If I could guess, I am sure your answer is yes because everyone is visited by the question why am I here at one point or another? Keep this in mind: if you have ever asked the question, "why am I here", or if you are asking that question right now, you are not alone. If you truly want to live life to its fullest, discovering your purpose is one of the biggest problems that we all must face.

I am so glad you are here right now because I have good news for you. There is a solution to knowing your God-given purpose! One of the many benefits available to Christians is to live a life that brings glory to God. But to do that we must pray, study the word of God, and stay in His will. God has left us with a wealth of wisdom, the examples of Jesus Christ and the Holy bible to help us. When we are feeling lost and facing our day with a lack of clarity, we need to remember who Jesus Christ is and what He says our purpose is in life. I truly believe a close relationship with God is the solution to discovering our purpose and exercising our gifts.

"For we are God's handiwork, created in Christ Jesus to do good works, which God prepared in advance for us to do." Ephesians 2:10

Throughout God's word we read about purpose. God has a plan for you and for me. God already knew we were not going to automatically know why we were put here, but He does expect us to seek Him to find out. We can and should ask Him and He will surely answer us. We are all called by God to live purposefully, courageously, confidently, and obediently, none of which is possible unless we are willing to recognize only God can help us discover why we are here. After all, He is the one who created us to do good works.

Initially, not knowing why you are here is not the absence of purpose; it is purpose that has said its prayer and decided to be revealed in you nevertheless by way of passion and sometimes through your biggest pains.

Purpose can be revealed through situations that hurt us the most. When you don't know your purpose not knowing can prevent you from doing many of the things that you never realized that God has charged you with to be a blessing to His people. Once you discover that you can live life on purpose with God you will see, the liberty we have in Jesus Christ. We can learn anything we need to learn because Jesus is with us and ruling in us. He said we can do all things with and through Him. It doesn't matter that you don't know right off; you can confidently go forward in faith trusting God. When you seek your purpose with faith in God, you might still feel the effects of not fully knowing, but the lack of clarity at the time really can't stop you in the end because God has a plan. Our gifts must eventually bow its knees to purpose simply because God created all of us with and for a purpose.

We all have a gift and some have many gifts. God gave everyone a unique purpose as to why they were created, but we all should have the same solution and that is to bring glory to God. We must put our faith in God and go forward doing what He created us to do. God's power is available to each of us, but it is only received through faith, which is vital because it's impossible to please God without it. If you're ready to reveal the gifts God gave you, you're in the right place. If you're ready to discover your purpose and learn to live a fulfilled, purposeful life, we believe you will receive the revelation knowledge you need. It is your adopted and inherited right as a son or daughter of God to live life to the fullest and to enjoy it while sharing your gift. Be expectant as you seek your life's purpose and be all God wants you to be, so you can help all that He has assigned you to help.

The authors of this book want to help you reveal the gifts God gave you. We want people to find purpose behind their pain and to show them that there's power behind their experiences and that they still have something to offer the world no matter what they have been through. Be expectant as you begin your journey to live your life on purpose. You want to be all that God wants you to be. You will be equipped to do all He wants you to do. If you read this divinely ordered and directed by God book with an open heart and focused mind, your life's purpose will be revealed.

DR. ONIKA L. SHIRLEY

ABOUT THE AUTHORS

DR. ONIKA L. SHIRLEY

Dr. Onika L. Shirley is an International Confidence and Procrastination Coach and Motivational Speaker. An accomplished professional who's led from a position in senior management in manufacturing, Dr. O is former president of the Greater Memphis Chapter of National Association of Professional Women for almost five years; former column writer and featured as a part of the cover story for Ordinary People Magazine; former contributing blogger for the Huffington Post; adjunct instructor at PCCUA of Phillips County; founder and director of Action Speaks Volume Orphanage Home in India; founder and director of Action Speaks Volume Sewing School in Pakistan; and coordinator for the State of Arkansas for God Head Prayer Ministry "Jesus Women" As a master storyteller, she develops her signature story to grow her business. Dr. O is an eight-time author and serial entrepreneur. She is a biological parent, adoptive parent, and foster parent and proud grandmother to baby Aubrey, who is her everything.

Dr. O earned three degrees including an undergraduate, a master's, and a doctorate degree. Of all her achievements, she is proudest of her profound faith in Christ as her personal Lord and Savior. Dr. O proves her selfless dedication to helping others by serving as a foster parent for the last 12 years and adoptive parent for the last 10 years. Dr. O overcame much adversity to reach this level of success. Through adversity, she has gained strength, motivation, and the resiliency to become the confidence and action coach that she is today.

Evangelist John Agbonifo

Evangelist John Agbonifo is a founder of centre for help initiative (NGO). This initiative has reached out to thousands of kids who are helpless in Edo state Benin city. John Agbonifo is a degree holder in public administration. He also attended World of Faith Bible Institute (WOBI). John is a songwriter, motivational speaker, and singer, but above all, he loves winning souls for Christ.

DR. ONIKA L. SHIRLEY

Jo Ann Lipscomb

Jo Ann Lipscomb is an amazingly anointed, gifted and transparent teacher, pastor, and mentor. She is passionate about pouring the word of God into others and walking side by side with them through their personal journey and development.

She is determined through her ministry, purpose, and calling to leave a lasting and positive legacy for her family, and through the disciplining of God's people, to make a difference in this culture. Through her local chapter, Chicktime Empowered, she is able to make this happen by, "Encouraging women to develop their passions and use their gifts to leave the world a better place for the next generation!"

She is the pastor of a "Host Church", New Beginnings Ministries, located at a local living center where they meet every Sunday. She also hosts a weekly radio show called, "Inspirational Moments" playing the latest in Christian and Gospel music. It airs Saturday's from 8-10 p.m. on San Marcos Community Radio Station, KZSM.org. She currently sits on the board of directors and heads their grant writing department.

Her first book, *Surrendered, Be It Unto Me*, is now available. Jo Ann has been appointed to the Human Services Advisory Board, which makes recommendations to the City Council for the allotment of funds to non-profit organizations in the San Marcos area.

Jo Ann is currently pursuing a BS degree in Religion/Christian Ministries from Liberty University. She has been married to her best friend Paul for 15 years and currently lives in San Marcos, TX, where they share a blended family of six children and nine grandchildren.

DR. ONIKA L. SHIRLEY

CHAPTER 1
OUR PURPOSE IS TO SERVE
DR. ONIKA L. SHIRLEY

For even the Son of Man did not come to be served, but to serve, and to give his life as a ransom for many."
Mark 10:45 (NIV)

    Many people in the world don't know why they are here and are easily distracted when things are not going the way they may have imagined them in their dreams. Day after day, week after week, month after month and year after year, people wake up feeling lost. People sometimes feel like they just don't know why God created them. They don't know what they like to do and even question their capabilities. Mark 10:45 is a great example for us to examine as we ponder who we are called to serve. I pray that God will fix in your mind and etch in your heart that you came to serve. There is somebody somewhere that God created just for you to improve in this life. The Son of Man came to serve the world because He had a purpose here on earth. He couldn't remain in heaven with an earthly assignment. His life, death, and resurrection should help us strengthen our faith in future grace to better understand why we are here. Through him, we should understand that we also have a purpose because no man is greater than their master.

We should also remember that Jesus served until his death. He sacrificed his life for the entire world and yes, that includes you and me. If we intend to live a life of service, we need to drink his cup, and share his baptism, namely, death. "The Son of Man came to give his life as a ransom for many." In both cases, he uses his death as an example of the kind of suffering and service that we are called to do today. Our purpose is a part of a radical call to discipleship and to make disciples all over the world. If we want to follow our Lord and Savior Jesus Christ and seek the glory of his kingdom, we must be prepared to suffer. Serving can be hard, but serving and following the example of Christ is worth it. The road that leads to life can be a hard road to travel every day, but it is possible to travel it with Christ. We must realize that there will only be a few that are truly willing to travel this road of suffering for the sake of Christ.

Jesus is the "living Word of God". In order for the bible to recognize its "living and active" status it must be read and lived in such a way that it serves the full, complete revelation of God we have in Christ. We must be active in our service and must be a living sacrifice. God's desire is for us to serve Jesus and serve His body. We have been given a helper and He helps us be good selfless helpers. The Holy Spirit empowers us to set aside our selfishness and teaches us to be selfless like Jesus, preferring others above ourselves. That kind of lifestyle starts in the mind, in the way we think. Our perspectives will change when you accept the fact that we are called to serve. As we think about our life and the purpose of it, it is a good idea to remember that we only have one life to live. Each of us will come face to face with God and we will be held accountable for everything we either did or did not do. God will be expecting an answer so create a life of service that will speak for you. While serving and seeking for your purpose in life you might find that it's difficult to do the right thing by willpower alone and serving like that will only last so long. We don't have the strength to do all the things that need to be done but the power of God and His amazing grace helps us bring all things to completion. This book of revealed purpose is full of encouragement and practical ways for you to be active, purposeful, confident, passionate, and filled with desire to serve.

I often think about the time. I think that every second of the day that goes by is one we will never get back. I'm sure you have already wasted enough time in your lifetime. I know I did. I thank God for His grace and His faithfulness towards us.

Since you now know at least one thing you were purposed to do, you shouldn't waste any more time living an unintentional life. We don't want to sit around waiting for things to happen for us; we should be making things happen. What we make happen for others God will make happen for us. As we live on purpose, serve God and the body of Christ. We have to make a conscious decision to take action. We think, we plan, and we serve from the heart. We don't serve with underlining motives that are not of God because in all that we do we want to make sure we are bringing glory to him. Your purpose may vary from season to season and those you are called to serve may vary. But the bible lets us know that we are called to serve God by serving others. "You, my brothers, were called to be free. But do not use your freedom to indulge to sinful nature; rather, serve one another in love." (Galatians 5:13)

We are told in the word of God that we are not saved by serving, but we are saved for serving. 2 Timothy 1:9 (NIV) reads "He has saved us and called us to a holy life—not because of anything we have done but because of his own purpose and grace. The grace was given to us in Christ Jesus before the beginning of time." We have a prerequisite for serving and must be set free by Christ Jesus. We can't serve in our sinful nature and be blessed by God. We must experience the transforming power of God's grace and the freedom of forgiveness so you will not find yourself serving for the wrong reasons: trying to be accepted by others; trying to earn others' approval; trying to ignore your pain; trying to overlook your own guilt; and trying to impress God. Service for the wrong reasons will leave you feeling empty, used, angry, and burned out in the end.

Serving God and His people is serious and we must not take the call and our purpose lightly. Everyone has a purpose and when anything is used inappropriately it is abused and there is little change in us. When we are not used for the purpose in which we were created we are being robbed of the privileges we could have and of the blessings we could be to others. We should appreciate the fact that we have been identified and called by name. God has created and called each of us with a specific name and for a pre-identified purpose. The Lord has called us by name and proclaimed that we are his son or daughter and that he is well pleased with us. Hearing your father tell you that he loves you and that he is well pleased are words that we all long for. So even if you didn't hear anything from your earthly father your heavenly father is speaking to you. We have been adopted into God's family and called to be followers and disciples of Jesus Christ. The Lord has a specific call for each of us. He had a specific purpose for you and for me from the very beginning. I am reminded of the call of Samuel's name in the middle of the night. Samuel had to be quiet to hear the voice of the Lord and we must do the same. Sometimes we don't hear or understand our call and our overall purpose seems to be unclear. Many don't have an idea why they are here, but the Lord doesn't appear to stop calling to us, until we answer the call. God knows what he wants you to do and in where he wants you to serve. God calls some into the ministry. The Spirit moves in the lives of others and calls them to be educators, public officials, financial counselors the whole gamut of vocations. Hearing our call and answering it gives us a sense of identity and a sense of purpose. So, what is your purpose? Who are you called to serve?

Have you heard God calling you in the middle of night? Have you answered the call and do you know that you are where God wants you to be, doing what God wants you to do, and that it is no coincidence that you are at this time and in this place reading this book? The world needs what you have and they need to hear the word of the Lord. The only way the people of the world will be redeemed is through our diligent service, our obedient actions and consistently doing what's right and just in the eyes of the Lord. You have a purpose. Let us be true to our purpose and honor the Lord in our lives because we all have been called to serve.

CHAPTER 2
EMBRACE YOUR LIFE'S PURPOSE
DR. ONIKA L. SHIRLEY

"And who know but that you have come to royal position for such a time as this" Esther 4:14

What is purpose? When you think about life purpose, it's the reason God created each of us and placed us here on earth. Our life purpose is always related to serving others and our gifts really are not for us. We must reveal our gift and embrace our purpose. We should see our circumstances, no matter what we have been through, as an opportunity for God to reveal his purpose for our lives. God did not create us waiting to find something for us to do; He created us with a plan already in mind. It's vital to build our faith while trusting God's plan.

You were strategically placed and God's plan is unique to you. God already had a strategy for you before you hit the scene on the earth. He had a plan to accomplish a desired end with everyone He made. The book of Esther is a perfect example of how one woman's unique and individual purpose was woven into God's big eternal strategy. Esther was strategically placed and so are you. Esther was reminded by her relative of her truth when he let her know she has come to royal position for such a time as this. Others may have thought her beauty put her in position but in reality it was her purpose that got her the promotion and placed into position. Purpose can place you in positions you never dreamed of or even imagined. Purpose can open doors that were shut and locked up. Esther realized that God placed her in her situation for a greater purpose than simply attaining high status, living in a beautiful environment, and wearing pretty clothes. She understood that she was strategically positioned to do something no one else could do.

Now, you must embrace your purpose and not view it as casual or simply existing. There are things that have been assigned to you specifically that others can't fulfill because they're not in your place and they were not created for your purpose. People may look at you and think you are in a certain position because of your education, your intelligence, or your connections. But that's not how our strategic God works. You are able to do what others have not been blessed to do because they are not in your place. Purpose can't wait for you to decide. Purpose is now. People are waiting on you. People want what you have and need what you have. God placed the answer to their needs inside you.

Are you ready to embrace your purpose? You can't just pass through purpose; you must embrace it. God has specifically positioned you to take part in his strategy. Whatever you're engaged in right now, is success waiting to happen. As we reflect back on the story of Esther, we see that at the hour of her purpose the king had not summoned Esther for 30 days. Although Esther was the wife of the king and she held a position, she was not in contact with the king every day. From her perspective her position was not perfect, but she had purpose. She was on a mission from God. She was connected to God's purpose of saving the Jewish people, risking her life, but she feared not and approached the king at just the right time. Esther 4:16 tells us that Esther said "When this is done, I will go to the king, even though it is against the law. And if I perish, I perish." This is a good time for you to consider your purpose. Purpose will sometimes require you to take risks. As you discover why you are here and who you are really here for, you must be willing to risk everything.

I know most believers in the United States don't live in cultures as Esther did that call for them to put their lives on the line. But people still do face persecution, the loss of their reputations, rejection and failure for simply trying to walk out their God-given purposes. Esther took risks and she could have lost her life by approaching the king without an invitation. The king could have rejected Esther. Being rejected because of your purpose may be the most unnerving of all the risks. When people are rejected, they tend to lose the courage and confidence to do what is needed. Have you ever talked yourself out of sharing the good news of Jesus Christ, applying for a position you knew you were qualified for, or starting up your dream business because you feared being rejected? You must overcome the risk of rejection to experience your life's purpose. You can't worry about the possibility of failure. When you work with God, you can't fail. We learn from Esther's limited perspective, failure was a possibility. God had a plan in place and He has one for you, too. God is so much bigger than any failure you could possibly face. Remember your purpose is central to His will. He causes all things to work together for your good. Sometimes it's only a matter of timing. You must be patient because God never fails. As you are seeking your purpose, you don't want to rush God. You must be willing to wait for God's appointed time. Some aspects of your purpose are not revealed until God's appointed time.

Have you ever been in the wilderness of the day-to-day hustle wondering what in the world God has in store for you? Have you thought He has something for everybody else, but He doesn't have anything for you? Be patient and know that your timing is not God's timing and God's ways are not your ways. You have it all wrong. Every day God blesses you to be on the earth you have something to do. I encourage you to stay focused and confident that as God's strategy unfolds your purpose will be revealed piece by piece. The story of Esther is a great example and it shows you what you must do to embrace your own God-given purpose. I don't know where you are in discovering and embracing your God-given purpose but wherever you are, see yourself as strategically placed. You are in place for a reason so connect your purpose to where you are today, you must be willing to risk everything for God, and be patient and willing to wait for the appointed time.

What steps are you willing to take to embrace your purpose? You can't worry about what others are doing or not doing. This is an individual journey. We all must embrace the purpose of why we are here. You have a purpose just like Esther had a purpose. When Esther walked in purpose she saved a nation. Inspire yourself to embrace your position and purpose in God's strategy. To fully embrace your purpose, you must fuel it with passion. Embrace the task God has assigned to you and realize that passion, a great attitude, and optimism can exert a positive impact on the lives of others. Your purpose is so much bigger than you. You were created to serve others and to bring glory to God while living a fulfilled life. God does indeed have a life purpose for you, and He will show it to you if you have ears to hear and eyes to see. Don't be stubborn and try to do things your way. God has the plan. Even if you don't know the next step, embrace it because God knows every step.

CHAPTER 3
WHAT GOD CREATED ME WITH
EVANGELIST JOHN AGBONIFO

Your gift and your passion towards your goals will reveal your purpose. You can't do well in an area you know little about. God created you with so much potential, talents, skills, and greatness. A man's gift makes room for him to access greatness. Don't worry about your small beginning. You will see how fast you have grown to become a pillar of hope to others. My experiences as a little boy taught me a lot. I grew up in a large family circle, polygamy, no attention for us by our parents, no love, and no parental care. I needed to start loving myself because what you love you invest in. Life will not give you what you want but what you demand. As a little boy, I had to work weekends to support my school. You have to be positive about what you do in life. If you start talking like a pauper you will only end up in a cage. Decisions determine destinies. Everything you are looking for is already inside of you.

People may not believe in you but believe in yourself. Trust God for what he can do. Nothing is impossible with him. Greatness is in service. You must serve before you can be served. Nobody is an island in this world. A lady became a widow with two children. Because of financial problems she had to quit but she didn't give up on her career. The kids are now adults and she has gone back to her study.

Determination pushes you fast to achieve your goals in life. Love is not in the eyes. Love is in the heart. What you put in is what you get in return. What people say about you don't really matter. What matters is your impartation towards people. A man was boasting about his money when someone asked him how many people have he been able to lift out of poverty in his community. The money you have made is not yours, it's for your mission. You have to be broad to understand this language. You are not only working for family alone. There are people outside of family who will benefit from your job. Listen to people and learn from them. Don't feel you know it all. Be careful not to make critical decisions when you are stressed or troubled. At such moments, you are beclouded by darkness and confusion. If you make decisions in that atmosphere, you can lose all the money that took you 10 years or more to build. You may spend 15 years regretting one decision you made in the dark. Program yourself for prosperity. You can become whatever you want to be in life, you can become who God has planned for you to be.

The size of your world is the size of your mind, but the size of your mind is determined by the size of your revelation. Revelation is what expands your inner world and your inner world expands your outer world. People ask me, "John, why do you believe in yourself?" I say, "I believe in myself because if I don't believe in myself nobody else will." Nobody can do better for me than I can do for myself. An ocean never runs dry because it has so much to give out. God saw that he couldn't walk in the dark, he had to bring light to an existence with the understanding that you need light in your daily activities. The bible tells us that God created everything for us. You must discover your calling to access your open heaven.

 A man's thought life is his center of gravity. You attract to yourself the quality of thought you carry inside of you. As a man thinks in his heart, so is he. You don't need to blame people for your failure. God has given us the right to succeed in this life. Work hard and pursue knowledge. Learn from people who have gone ahead of you in life to successfully discharge the mandate you are given in life. You need people to help you achieve these goals. You may not become your best in life until you hook up with your destiny helpers. Some may appear unkempt but they are destiny helpers, so do not despise people when they appear poor or not what you expect them to appear in person.

Don't make your world so small by having small thoughts because your spiritual controls your physical. People will laugh at you when you begin but relax because God has not given us the spirit of fear. Don't let people feel sorry for your new start up. Tell yourself you can do it better even when it appears things aren't going well. You must trust God in your journey of life.

WHAT YOU NEED TO KNOW ABOUT YOUR DOMINION RIGHT

- If you see the invisible, you can see the visible.
- If you can imagine it, you can see it.
- If you dream it, you can see the reality of it.
- If you allow God to involve you, he can strengthen you.

Every resource you need to accomplish what God has sent you forth to do here on earth is already inside of you. There are dominion prayers that bring out your hidden gifts and talents. A man who is blind physically is better than the man who is blind spiritually and the man who is blind mentally. A boy who was always dreaming of entering an airplane in Benin City here in Nigeria took a bold step by going to the airport and narrowly entered the tire of an airplane to fly out. He was on every TV station in Nigeria which led to him receiving a scholarship from the government. If you can imagine it, you can do it. The people we celebrate today give their time, their strength, sacrifices and money, so be ready to sacrifice and to give of your precious time, too. The bible tells us about a prodigal son who wasted all that his dad gave him. If God blesses you and gives you money, you should learn to have a manager mentality because it will take you to your promise land. You need the wisdom of God to direct you to the right place where you can excel in life.

I didn't come from a wealthy family, but I believed in such a manner to make a difference. I started a center for help initiative because I believe in helping people improve their lives. Center for help is a non-governmental organization that helps street kids, widows, HIV patients, and victims of rape in my locality. As a little boy, a lot of girls where abused in my community. Don't let your past dictate your future. Today center for help is a reality organization for the less privileged in our society. Thinking small will limit your progress in life. Because I know I'm above and not beneath, my father God owns everything in this world. Today people celebrate mother Teresa all over the world because she sacrificed so much for poor kids and hopeless people. She gave her money and she gave of her time.

DR. ONIKA L. SHIRLEY

CHAPTER 4
ACTIVATING YOUR VISION
EVANGELIST JOHN AGBONIFO

Activating your dreams and vision means you have to discover for yourself what God has gifted you with. You must pray that God show you pathways to your talents and gifts. You may have gifts lying dormant inside you. God created the whole universe, so as a son of God, you have the ability to create or bring into existence whatever you desire. Every great vision starts small. You can actually succeed if you care about what it takes. When you neglect prayer, you neglect victory in your life. A comedian who goes to a show for just one hour gets paid $1million. This is talent on display. When he was asked what drives him, he said, "I believe in myself and I trust God for a change." For him, becoming a great comedian was not easy to bring to pass, but he had to sell out shows to support himself.

In the journey of giving birth to your visions, there are obstacles, but be courteous and patient. God didn't bring you here for small things; he brought you here for big things. If you don't fight, nobody will fight for you. If nobody encourages you encourage yourself. Nigeria is so blessed with resources, but our leaders are so corrupt that in the midst of abundance a lot of the citizens can't eat three square meals a day. If you allow greed to step into your life you will never love compassionately. You must make that decision, but it might not be an easy decision. No pain. No gain. What you do perfectly well takes you to your promise land.

Joseph was sold out by his people, he was sold to slavery, but they didn't know they sold him out for greatness and prosperity. What is fighting you is also afraid of you. Learn how to resist it. The bible speaks of resisting the devil and he will flee from you. You can be a gift to your generation but undiscovered if you don't know your calling in life. Prayers and fasting can open your eyes of understanding to see when your gift is based on your area of gift and talents. Humble people so that people can also humble you, respect your followers and leaders too. God's family is the largest family in the world, a family that has an ability to expand into different branches as a united family of God's children. Jesus is your elder brother, he's the first born in the house. As the father treasures the relationship with the son, so also he values his relationship with us.

We are meant to conform to the image of the son, just as the son's image of God the father. We too are the image of the father. God came into this world as a man named Jesus. He manifested in the flesh and was seen of men and of angles. He was justified in the spirit, preached unto Gentiles and received up into glory. As for you, fulfil your purpose for which God sent you here on earth in Jesus name. Amen. A lot of folks have died with their talent and gifts because they were too busy with other things that were not in line with their calling, when you don't know your purpose in life you will tour for nothing with no result. If you die without fulfilling God's purpose for your life, you are a disgrace to God almighty. He loaded you with so much to come utilize here on earth. Remove every limitation you have placed on yourself by your wrong thinking. Think big and eat well. Dress well, too. The future is bright if you can see it. God's word has told you

all things are yours and you have an inheritance in Christ Jesus. Amen. Value who you are. All I know to say is, "I can do all things through Christ that strengthens me."
What takes place on your inside plays a more significant role than your external reality. Mistakes are killers. Laziness can't fetch you wealth just grow up and become wise and smart in life. God wants your destiny to show forth even if nobody can see it. Yet, he loves you so much. I wish above all things so you may prosper and be in health and help your generation.

We are heavenly citizens on an earthly adventure. We are here presently just like our elder brother, Jesus was once on the earth on an assignment. When we accomplish our assignment here, we go home to our father in heaven. The supernatural should not be alien to you. You are a spirit being, and you are created with the image of God. You are an offspring of a deity.

CHAPTER 5
DISCOVERING YOUR PURPOSE
JO ANN LIPSCOMB

I found out one night, while sitting in a dismal state on my bed, "Discovering Your Purpose," is a discovery made while searching the heart of God. That night will forever be etched in my mind because that is when I died to self and gave my life to Christ. That night I found out God had all I needed to want to live again and not give up on myself because of mistakes, bad choices, and negative words others had to say about me. Sitting on my bed that night my conversation with God was, "If you don't step in and do something, I don't know what the final decision will be for my life tonight."

Crying out to God that night was the wisest thing I could have done, I had come to a point where I had depleted all options, tried everything and asked everyone I could think of for their opinions of how to stop my life from spinning totally out of control. The only thing I had left was to go to a God I had little knowledge of expect what I heard about Him in church, the God I saw my parents so committed and dedicated to, the God I read about from time to time and the same God I knew had intervened in certain situations in different times in my life. This was the God I found myself crying out to – to save me! And, this was the God who answered, "Jo Ann, Minister My Word."

Yeah right! For a split second I really felt that God was playing word games with me. I found myself getting a little angry because I thought maybe God wasn't interested in me or my life at all. So, the only answer I could give him that night was, "I don't know you well enough to minister your word," and to my surprise His answer was, "Exactly. Now allow me to introduce myself to you in a way that you will never forget." I found out that night knowing God through going to church only, through others, including my parents, wasn't good enough. There had to be a point in my life when I had to get to know Him for myself. This was the night, the beginning of a lifelong relationship with Him that had to be personal, truthful, transparent, and all about Him. Instead of dying by myself that night, I died to myself and found life again in Christ, a life that will forever touch and change the lives of others, a life that will never be my own again, and a life that will forever glorify my Lord and Savior until I meet Him in eternity. God's word in Hebrews 13:5-6 says, that He will never leave me nor forsake me, that He will be with me forever,"(NIV) I hold on to and live through that truth, a truth that will never again find me sitting on my bed not knowing who I am and to whom I belong. It's a truth that is currently carrying me through the good, bad and ugly in life and assures me that no matter what I encounter along the way, He is the one leading, guiding, and protecting me as I allow Him to use me for His glory and to serve others. I made a defining moment decision that night that has changed my life forever. It has given God permission to live His life through me! This was the pivotal point in my life when purpose was revealed.

Stop Trying To Figure God Out

My first encounter with God came with a lot of questions and trying to figure out how He was going to equip me to, "Minister His Word". My mind was so blown away by this encounter that the entire room was spinning. I felt like the after effects of too many Long Island Teas lying on my bed that night, except I hadn't drunk anything, I had only an encounter that left me with more questions than answers, that left me, for a split second, wondering if God has stopped by the wrong house to talk to the wrong person. I couldn't, for the life of me, understand how God was going to use a person who had made so many embarrassing and stupid mistakes. If I wanted nothing else to do with my own life, how could he possibly have plans and a purpose for me?

How could He use someone who kept finding love in all the wrong places time and time again, who was once beaten repeatedly and treated like my life didn't matter, who subjected her kids to all this mess and made this kind of living a lifestyle she could never see her way out of except to sit on her bed and contemplate ending everything? What plans could He have for a, "hot mess" like me? And, how was He going to accomplish what He had shown me in dreams and visions? Could He turn this mess of a person into someone He was not embarrass to use? After coming out of an abusive marriage, I had used the clubs, house parties, happy hour, and other men as objects to numb the pain this type of relationship can cause, until I could finally find and live a life worth something. Until then, all these things would have to continue until something or someone better came alone. That night, little did I know, Jesus was my someone and something with an eternal worth and forever love He had tailor made just for me.

Isaiah 55:8-9 (NIV) is a constant reminder that His ways and thoughts are higher than mine. In other words, you can spend a lifetime with God and never fully understand how He does what He does and how He works His will through us. But you can rest assure He knows the way and the outcome. By allowing God to lead, I learned how to trust in Him and never look back or regret my decision to follow Him. God chose to come to me at a time when the consequences of my sins had finally caught up with me and I had no place to go but to myself for a quick end or to Him for an eternal purpose.

The children of Israel found themselves in the same predicament when they chose to sin against God and not listen to any of His warnings before Babylon conquered and took them into slavery. As they were walking into captivity, God reminded them in the middle of their suffering and consequences of their sin, that they still belonged to Him. Jer. 29:11: "For I know the plans I have for you," declares the Lord, "plans to prosper you and not to harm you, plans to give you hope and a future." (NIV) God reminded them, like He reminded me, that His plans and purpose for my life did not end because of the mistakes I've made. His purpose and promises are always yes and amen. It's up to us to turn, repent and accept what God has to offer. I had to understand that what He told Jeremiah is what He's telling me today. Jer. 1:5 says, "Before I formed you in the womb I knew you, before you were born I set you apart. I appointed you as prophet to the nations." (NIV) His plan and purpose was established long before I made it to this earth and long before I knew myself, therefore His plan and purpose is for Him to accomplish and not for me to try to accomplish His will for my life on my own.

No More Shame

If we allow it to, shame from our past and present situations has the power to totally shut down our lives. There are times when I look back on the life I led before Christ came and changed everything, and if I concentrate on the negatives too long, shame will creep in and try to steal my joy, have me question God's plan for me and make me feel like everyone is looking at me with disgust. It will have me thinking, no one is going to listen to what I have to say and the things God has me doing is just making a fool out of me. If I'm not careful I will allow these negative thoughts to consume me and cause a distraction which will put everything God is doing, through me, on hold.

My escape...

One day, God let me know that He has the ability and power to use everything regarding my life, past, present and future as His platform to reach back and touch, strengthen, and change the lives of many. All I have to do is stand on His promises and keep moving forward. He reminded me of the conversation He had with Peter in Luke 22:31-32, "Simon, Simon, Satan has asked to sift you as wheat. But I have prayed for you, Simon, that your faith may not fail. And when you have turned back, strengthen your brothers." (NIV) This scripture can be a constant reminder of the evil intent Satan has in mind for us and the assurance that Christ is going to battle on our behalf. If we keep this in mind and concentrate on God's word, shame will never have a foothold in our lives and never have the power to shut us down, destroy us, or doubt God's love.

That encounter was over 20 years ago but when I look back I see now how God used that encounter to begin the process of shaping, strengthening, and developing a personal relationship with me that He uses to move me forward and through the plans He has prepared for my life. The visions and dreams I mentioned earlier were to show me what His intentions were and, "ministering His word," was not impossible through Him. Through these dreams and visions, He was able to show me the crowd He was placing in me in front of me. I was able to hear the messages He had prepared for me to preach, I saw people being saved, set free, and healed and even though I saw myself as the one ministering and laying on hands, the voice I heard was His. This went on for 90 days non-stop, it was the most intimate, intense, and unforgettable time of my life. Shame has no place on God's platform prepared for me.

What Makes You Better Than Me?

When it's time for us to go through difficulties and pain, whether it's our fault or caused by someone else, we tend to create our own pity party and expect Christ to join us. I have had many times like that. But this time a fellow minister decided to take their anger and frustration out on me because they felt overlooked at a women's event. I almost passed out from disbelief, embarrassment, and confusion. I went to God and He made sure my emotional needs were seen by directing me to another minister friend.

He also let me know that there was no need to address the issue. He would take care of it and deal with her but He also dealt with me.

As I was sitting in my car hurt and caught up in my emotions, He quietly whispered in my spirit, "What Makes You Better Than Me?" At first, I thought I had heard Him wrong so I murmured the usual Hmmm? To my amazement He repeated Himself, this time with an attitude, "What Makes You Better Than Me?" For the first time I couldn't think of how to answer such a strange question. So I did the normal thing, I sat and listened to what He had to say. I can say that I was not ready for His response but I was curious. He reminded me of how the world rejected Him, cursed, beat, called Him crazy, called Him a liar, turned their backs on Him, whipped, spat, tried to shame Him by disrobing Him, nailed Him to a cross, placed thorns on His head, pierced Him in the side, and left Him to die. He allowed me to see how the crowd accepted evil (Barabbas) and rejected truth and righteous (HIM) and how not even His own accepted Him as the Son of God. If the world hated me, and now I live inside of you, what makes you think they're not going to hate you? What makes you think you're any better than me?

I was floored, but in the middle of my emotional breakdown I found strength and began to count it all joy to be able to share in Christ's suffering in a way that allowed Him to comfort me. John 15: 18-25 says, "If the world hates you, keep in mind that it hated me first. If you belonged to the world, it would love you as its own. As it is, you do not belong to the world, but I have chosen you out of the world. That is why the world hates you. Remember what I told you: 'A servant is not greater than his master. If they persecuted me, they will persecute you also. If they obeyed my teaching, they will obey yours also. They will treat you this way because of my name, for they do not know the one who sent me. If I had not come and spoken to them, they would not be guilty of sin; but now they have no excuse for their sin. Whoever hates me hates my Father as well. If I had not done among them the works no one else did, they would not be guilty of sin. As it is, they have seen, and yet they have hated both me and my Father. But this is to fulfill what is written in their Law: 'They hated me without reason." (NIV)

Don't ever think that you're above your master. Know that because they hated Him first, they will hate you without a cause and will try to destroy everything about you that's righteous and pure. But also know since Jesus went through suffering and persecution before you, He is the one you run to when you find yourself treated wrongly by the world. God is so caring and He makes sure we are aware of our adversary's plans but at the same time He lets us know the plans He has for us. John 10:10 says, "The thief comes only to steal and kill and destroy; I have come that they may have life, and have it to the full." (NIV) God lets us know there is a distinct difference between the hate Satan has for us and the love He has for those who belong to Him.

After 90 days of visions and dreams, Jesus thought it

necessary to send me back to a difficult place, to mature, strengthen and develop the leader He had called me to become. Because of this place, I can relate to people who have been so hurt in the church that they don't want to go back, I can relate to Jesus when He said, "my own knew me not," and I can relate to not being accepted by people who you felt should be so happy you have decided to come out of the world and accept Christ as your Lord and Savior. When they showed me the opposite and wished me back into the world, I learned how important it was for Jesus to change me from the inside out. By this I mean I learned how to follow and obey as the Holy Spirit lead even when others fought so hard against me.

I was called to, "Minister His Word," and the process I went through may have been difficult but, He still allowed me to get through it. For me it was on the job training from the beginning. There was no time to sit down. Christ had a plan and I had wasted enough time already with foolishness. When He led me back to a place of hardship, it was for my advantage not my failure. When I came out two years later, it was for my comeback not setback and when He placed forgiveness in my heart, it was for my eternity with Him not damnation away from Him. If I had to do that difficult time of process all over again, I wouldn't change a thing, I'd "gird up my loins" and trust in God to see me through.

Because of the difficult process God saw fit to allow me to go through in the beginning. When it came time to show restraint as this minister was disrespecting and making me the butt of her jokes at a table full of people, I walked away knowing God was walking with me and He would fight this battle for me. I walked away with my integrity intact, without ruining my witness, or damaging my ministry. I walked away bruised but not broken and opened to what God had to say. I walked away with peace and joy that God was in control from beginning to end. I walked away the leader He had spent so much time shaping me into. I found that day, Philippians 4:13 which says, "I can do all things through Christ who give me strength," (NIV) even if it meant to, "walk away." Don't be surprised or caught off guard when the world, including the church, decides to come against you. Remember they came against Jesus first. If it didn't destroy Him, it won't destroy you. Try to use these difficult times and situations to strengthen you where you're weak, mature you in areas you're still immature and more like Christ where you still allow flesh to lead.

Purpose Lived

My bedroom encounter gave God a chance to show me what His purpose looked like and that nothing was too hard for Him to bring into fruition. I know now that living through the planned purpose of God is worth going through any and everything in order for you to come out as the person he needs to fulfill His vision for "such a time as this!" Esther wasn't the only one God had purposed to save His people. He has purposed us to do the same. According to Matthew 28:19, "Therefore go and make disciples of all nations, baptizing them in the name of the Father and of the Son and of the Holy Spirit." (NIV)

We are to go and offer salvation to all who will listen and accept. If you're not sure about your purpose, pause for a minute and pray for God to reveal to you what plans He has for you. He will not disappoint, He will answer and you will become Gods purpose on purpose for a purpose. As soon as you pray, keep an open mind and allow God to begin speaking to your spirit what's on His heart and mind for you. You will find out quickly that prayer is a dialogue not a monologue. He will and does speak back. Then accept everything He says and shows you, even if you don't understand how He's going to accomplish it all. Just go with the flow and don't resist.

Purpose Lived is a life in progress, a life God is currently using for His glory. It's a life lived the way God has intended it to be and a life that people are benefiting from and finding God through. If you're wondering what this kind of life looks like, let me brag on what God is doing in my life and the life of others who are crazy enough to say yes to His way and yes to His purpose.

Purposed Revealed is seeing, living and being a part of the calling, plan and purpose He has tailor made just for you. I'm proud to have accomplished so much and at the same time knowing God is not finished with me. I anxiously step into whatever He has next for my life and I'm mindful to invite others to join me if God approves and they accept. There are areas in my life, character, personality and disposition God is still working on but I refuse to allow a few flaws to slow me down or stop me from following Christ.

I have refused to put any limitation on God and just allow myself to discover something I never knew about me until God introduced a new gift. When God places television as a way He wanted to spread the Gospel through me, I panicked and called myself not talking to Him for a while thinking this would change His mind. Not the God I serve, He just touched the heart of a person who knew the ends and outs of TV and partnered us together. Then He somehow let everyone know I needed guests and the flood gates opened and never closed until my last show. I even had people ask if I could assist in writing, directing and being a guest on their shows. God showed me that nothing was impossible for Him if I would only believe and keep moving forward.

When I tried to talk God out of using me to speak anymore, due to medication affecting my heart and speech, He showed me that He had and still has a keen sense of humor. He not only increased my speaking engagements, put me as Pastor of a host church at the living facility but He also opened up and opportunity for me to host my very own radio show. It was like He was saying, "Now how's that for sitting down?" I don' think so! The moment I think I know what God is going to do in a certain situation, He does the complete opposite. The scripture He keeps placing in my heart is Isa. 55:9, "As the heavens are higher than the earth, so are my ways higher than your ways and my thoughts than your thoughts." (NIV)

Trying to put God in a box or limit His purpose in your life is a waste of time and energy, just go with the flow and enjoy discovering new things about yourself. You will find yourself having a different perspective regarding your abilities, desires, and accomplishments. Like me, you will begin to be comfortable living in the, "Next" of what God has on His agenda for your life and your legacy will be, "Me and My House Will Serve the Lord!" Joshua 24:15 (NIV)

As you can see, I've come a long way since my first encounter with God and because He's not finished with me, I still have a long way to go serving Him and blessing others. I pray that this chapter made clear the importance of allowing God to develop a personal and intimate relationship with you so that when your purpose is revealed it will not be hard to let God, "take the wheel," in your life. As you can see, God's purpose is limitless and so is your potential to succeed and be successful in what God has called and equipped you to do.

CHAPTER 6
LIVING ON PURPOSE
DR. ONIKA L. SHIRLEY

God has a will and purpose for each of us, and His desire is that we make the choice to choose His will. When God created you He did so with a plan just for you and He promises to guide you every step of the way if you're willing to follow His plan. God will only guide us, but He will never force us or trick us into doing anything. Each day that God allows breath to be in our bodies is indeed a gift and we have the choice to value and enjoy it. One of the ways to show God you value the day is to use every day purposefully, not procrastinating or allowing yourself to be pulled by circumstances that you cannot change or control. Everyday can count towards the will of God if we learn to live it on purpose rather than not knowing what the day will bring. We should not allow the fiery darts of life to distract us and pull us in other directions that are not of God and not in His will. In the very beginning, God gave man authority, dominion, and instructed him to be fruitful and to multiply. God wants us to use the resources He provided and make the day count.

There are a lot of people willing to make the day count, but many don't know what to do. Some people have not discovered their purpose and find themselves asking the question, "Why am I here?" and "What is God's will for my life?" If we don't know why we are here, it may be that we are not asking the right questions. We may seek God for answers to our questions about materialistic possessions and circumstances in our lives but overlook and fail to ask Him what He will have us to do. Who will he have you to serve? Where will He have you to go? Questions about our circumstances are important to God but they are not priority questions. Our Lord and Savior Jesus told us what to ask and to seek in one of my favorite scriptures, Matthew 6:33, which says: "But seek first his kingdom and his righteousness, and all these things will be given unto you as well" Matthew 6:33 (NIV)

God wants us to seek His kingdom for deep things. His desire is that all men would come to the saving knowledge of Jesus Christ, and through Christ come to establish a personal and intimate relationship with Him. When we get to know God deeply, intimately, and personally, we will more than likely know the answers to life circumstances and to our questions of why we are here. We must have a determined mind to know God and not just know about God. When we know Him, we will desire to know what he desires of us. We should not allow materialistic things and other people to be more important to us than God himself. God created us with a purpose in mind and a plan to fulfill it. We just need to seek His face and follow His plan. Knowing anything requires studying and a willingness to take heed to the lessons being taught. I will warn you now to be patient because learning can sometimes take a while and it takes effort. As we are working on living on purpose and knowing why God created us, be patient with an open heart and a desire to learn so God can teach us.

When we seek God's face and know His word, we will find many answers to our questions regarding our daily lives and God's desire for us in His plan. I encourage you to diligently seek God by studying His word and stop casually looking for Him because you may pass right by Him. Did you know God is everywhere and capable of helping everybody at the same time. He talks about looking over the least of these because we might be overlooking Him. As we live a purposeful life God's will is that we learn to love him, others, and ourselves. God is so good and He is so worthy of the honor and all the praise. Living on purpose requires love and when we have the love of God down in our hearts it makes walking and living on purpose fulfilling. It won't be perfect, but it will be worth it.

Time waits on no man or woman so the time is now for you to do what you were created to do. Every person should long to live up to their full God given potential. When you live up to your full God given potential you will find that life will extend an entirely different experience. It feels good to discover and understand what drives you to do the things you do to bring glory to the God of the Heavens. You may find your purpose wrapped up in your current struggles or through some of your past pains. Nietzsche said, "He who has a why to live for can bear almost any how." Now that is the power of purpose. Once you get it and completely embrace the power behind your purpose, lives will be impacted and completely changed forever. Persecution, struggles, and unimaginable situations will be superseded by purpose. Although there are weapons created against us and things that were designed to destroy us, purpose is what gives us the strength to pick up the broken pieces and put our lives back together. Purpose teaches us that weapons are formed but they will not prosper. When you decide to live on purpose, you will be more willing to share your pain and your past rather than hiding it. You discover you are here for a time such as this.

You will no longer sit back feeling sorry for yourself and asking God why a certain thing happened to you. Instead, you will embrace every piece of your pain and be willing to pick up the pieces to heal yourself and others. There was a lesson taught in what you went through. We don't always ask to learn everything, but we can use what was said and what was done to help ourselves and others in the future. Your purpose is about serving not being served. It's about giving and not getting. Purpose is counterintuitive so remember what you make happen for others God will make happen for you. Living on purpose is intentional. Jesus is a great example of living an intentional and on purpose life. He came from glory on purpose for a purpose, and He was diligent in fulfilling His purpose. When people wanted Him to stay in one place, He let them know He had to stick to the plan of His purpose. I'm encouraging you not to allow well-meaning people to prevent you from fulfilling your purpose in life even though they might care about you. Their plans are often selfish and based on what's best for them and not according to the plans of God for you. Jesus came to be our example. He taught the gospel. He paid for our sins by way of the cross. He came to destroy the work of enemy, to give us an example to live by, to be an example of how we are to serve, and to fulfill the law. Jesus did the things mentioned here and so many others things that were not recorded. We are told in the bible "very truly I tell you, whoever believes in me will do the works I have been doing, and they will do even greater things than these, because I am going to the Father." John 14:12 (NIV). Purposefully follow the examples of the light and do not allow darkness to overtake you. Be purposefully engaged in the things that are right and in the things that will bring glory to God.

Living on purpose requires to you be intentional. Life will come against you, but when you live a life of purpose you will choose to respond differently. You are uniquely made for certain task and to work with a specific group of people that was assigned to you and you only. No one will ever be able to do what God gave you the way He gave it to only you. They might be able to do something but your DNA is DNA and your purpose is just like your DNA. Seek your purpose diligently and allow God to work with you and through you. When you seek His face, He will guide your feet and order every step He desires for you to take. The steps you take and the moves you make will bring glory to God. You shouldn't allow situations and circumstances to take you off course and away from God's plan. When you follow God's plan, He will show you His power and you will make a lasting impact on the world. You want to be known for the works you did long after you leave the earth and the meaningful differences you made in the lives of others. While living life on purpose, you want to cherish every moment and seek to live your life without regrets because you know during your waking and working moments you did what you were called to do.

Here are a few things you can do to live your life on

purpose:
- Give your life wholeheartedly to the things you're passionate about.
- Strive to follow the best example ever given by Jesus Christ to live an "On Purpose Life" and actually fulfill it.
- Choose today to seek God's face and His kingdom so you will know your purpose, if you have not already discovered it.

DR. ONIKA L. SHIRLEY

CHAPTER 7
BE FRUITFUL AND MULTIPLY
EVANGELIST JOHN AGBONIFO

God said be fruitful and multiply, it means go and do what eyes have not seen. In my little experience in this life, I have seen God change the stories of people. God is saying, I have loaded you with so much potential and wisdom to change your world. If you can't see it, you can't access it. God has blessed you so you can be a blessing, too. I heard a story of a woman who was married for 20 years, but no child and her husband trusted God for a child. People mocked them. She and her husband trusted God for a change of story. The man kept saying God created us to be fruitful not barren. God visited them with triplets and their story changed. Patience will destroy your affliction, so trust God for total freedom. Bill Gates has given so much to Africa. He saw the reason God blessed him so he was excited about helping people. African leaders are so greedy that is why most African countries are undeveloped. Greed will not let them help their people. They want to acquire so much for themselves that they forget that life begins when people are happy and their dreams are fulfilled in life.

Think about this... what you are dying for, another person is giving out happily. A man who is greedy causes his generation to suffer lack and want because what you sow you will also reap.

Whenever greed is stronger than compassion, it will not make them better people. When you chase shadows, you will not get results. It only happens when you go after reality. You don't help people because of what you want them to do for you; we help people so they can do well in life.

Life is not measured by how much you own because one day you will die and those things don't go with you. But your legacy lives on. Your impartation will speak when you leave. You are a footprint of God. Dr. Onika Shirley discovered her purpose for why God brought her here. She is sharing her gift with millions of people all around the world.

A business without profit is like wasting precious time. Those who feel they should make other people unhappy to gain treasure will regret their lives. You can't make people go through difficulties and expect a good life. As you read this book, your testimony will be evidence to all to see this year, in Jesus name. Amen.

When you follow the wrong people and their bad attitude, you become a carrier of bad influence. Be careful how you chose your friends. There is a proverb that says, "Show me your friends and I will tell you who you are." What you do every day you become a product of. If you are a furniture maker and you treat your customers well, they will definitely recommend you to a lot of people. One good turn deserves another. A son starts what he sees he's father doing. He practices his father's footsteps. Somebody who think he/she can't succeed until he steals another person's money will never be a better person in life. It's God that gives you the power to make wealth not man. Everything you need God has already given it freely to you. The Bible says, and this same God who takes care of me, will supply all your needs from his glorious riches, which have been given to us in Christ Jesus.

People will do well and shine when they see the right soil to sow. Everyone has something to give and it's only when you don't recognize what you have to give that you find yourself holding on to what you have. But there is always something to give to God's people.

HOW DO I BECOME FRUITHFUL AND MULTIPLY
- God said it already be fruitful.
- Obey God's word.
- Don't sow in bad soil.
- Be productive.
- Partner with what is good.

CHAPTER 8
YOU ARE A SPECIAL SEED
EVANGELIST JOHN AGBONIFO

You are a special seed God brought into this earth. You came from your biological parents, but you are a spirit being. Even Jesus was here on earth through physical means by Mary. He was conceived spiritually but came physically. Wisdom is the principal thing but you need knowledge and understanding before you can manifest your wisdom through your action. Wisdom is reflected by your actions. You must educate your mind and because we are in a world of technology, we must learn that, too. I started writing songs when I was about 13 years old. I got it early but my parents didn't nurture the gift.

The seed you have must be nurtured to grow and produce the harvest of your destiny, which is the that purpose God planted for you here on earth. You must grow from being a baby to a mature adult to grow in your God-given gift area of your life. God had arranged Joseph and Mary to help protect Jesus until he had matured, otherwise Herod would have killed him. He told Joseph to take the baby to Egypt. When your dream is still young you have to protect it and nurture it to maturity. The world is full of battles and challenges. Be strong, stand, and do exploits in your area of endeavor as a champion in life. We exist to grow together as a team, brothers and sisters. We all need each other to survive in this world because the greatest achievement in life is making people's lives better. If you don't invest in your career and in people's lives, you will soon start regretting your life. People created by God come through with human effort. So anything good can come from God's creation.

Even in scientific programming there is a time that the information that is being coded into the computer must be allowed to load. The command has been given to the computer, but it requires the loading time to enter and settle permanently in the computer. If you stop the loading before it is completed, you will not have a successful installation of that program. If I can start thinking right, I will see the import of it and work hard because all hard work brings profit. Be open to everyone so you can also learn from people who have gone ahead of you, even when people don't trust God and believe in themselves. In Africa, so many people have done things on their own without government support. We already grow up in the hard way of life. A government that doesn't treat its people right, has allowed greed to step in. When you treat people right and love them unconditionally, they will see you as their messiah. Weakness can't have a final say in your life. Let your inner mind rise up in strength and wisdom.

When something happens to you it is for you to learn from it, that's when you receive insight for another level. A friend once told me good people don't last. I told him that it is not true. I said to him good people leave lasting memories behind. I said when you say good people don't last that is an incorrect statement; they last very well. The worst thing that can happen to a man is to be under the influence of the power of darkness. Your faith has to grow to nurture your vision. The giant in you has to grow so don't ever look down on yourself. Your seed has the ability to rise inside of you.

WHY SOME AFRICAN MEN DON'T GROW

Some Africa men will marry four wives or more. In my own side of the country, it can even be more. I thank God for civilization. These guys believe when you have many kids you have a good workforce. They think these kids can help them with their farms so they don't to send them to school. A lot of our grannies didn't go to school either, most were uneducated people. Some of them were taken by western world folks for slavery. How can you marry four wives and expect to make progress in life? You can only do so much. The wives normally have an agenda for cooking for their husband. Some men found out marrying four wives was not normal. You can only sell what you know is good for others to use. Don't send bad signals to people and always try to improve lives instead of killing lives. Your wife is not your slave but your help mate, you need to love your wife unconditionally, then a lot of these Africa men were treating their wives like slaves. But in my locality, civilization has come to stay, even though some Africa men still practice polygamy in some Africa countries. Some even abuse their wives and lock them up in a room for days.

When you don't learn good things, you produce bad things. You can only give back what you have been given. If you know what God has called you for, you will prepare yourself for it. Your calling might be different from mine. When God sends you a message he will provide resources, but you have to prepare yourself. If he called you into ministry you have to study Christian books, tapes, and go to bible school. You have to be mentally sound and be fit for the job. There is more inside of you, more than the mineral resources we have here on earth, God created you with his own image and good can come out of you. Remember, God created man. If God kept quiet allowing you to pass through the storm, He is also there to see you triumph. Know your worth or you will fall for something cheap. You can't find purpose until you discover what God has called you to do. Your mouth is your starting of destiny. Every human being you see is a magnet, and knowledge is the key that opens doors. No matter the challenge that comes your way, you can overcome it. Your ability to stand for what you want is inside you already. Imagine knowing that your mission was to complete a journey that even Moses could not accomplish. God reminded Joshua to be brave in the task laid ahead of him. Simply imagine the future challenges within this advice but Joshua faced his mission with courage and strength. In a frightening situation, a natural impulse is to grab someone close. People seek comfort by clinging to others. Leaders are not any different when an intimidating challenge appears. If you are new in your position of leadership or you are a seasoned leader facing a new task, your courage can be attacked by fear. In those times, be reminded that you can be bold and courageous because God is with you. You do not have to back out of a challenge because you are intimidated, you don't have to face your fear alone. Reach for God to capture courage and stand strong. I urge you today to share your ideas with wise colleagues. You may gain the confidence you need to conquer your fear. Your vision is the promise of what you shall one day be. Do you know God has promised to give you the desires of your heart?

Your heavenly father knows better than anyone what you were created to do on earth. Begin to pay attention today to what really matters to you by honoring your personal preferences in small ways. When you are presented with a choice, stop saying it does not matter or I don't care. Allow yourself to choose from your heart.

Inside of every one of us is the seed of the person we were meant to become. If we have hidden this seed as a result of what we were told by others, our parents, teachers, coaches, role models or mentors, we will never have a chance to blossom when we lose touch of what we really want. We end up becoming dead to our desires. We sometimes do not dare to dream because somewhere along the line, someone told us not to. Someone once said, the poor man is not he who is without a dream. Don't give up on that God-given dreams. The road may be rough but you will win in the end. Time will tell you how fast you have grown to become a better person in life. Life will not give you what you want to see happen in your life, but believe in yourself. You are the best person to encourage yourself and trust God completely. The difference between the runner who wins and the runner who loses is their motivation for the race. Trophies are not enough to provide the tenacity needed for a marathon race. Integrity, compassion and courage can be the fuel that keeps the runner in the race until the finish line. An inner motivation must fuel the leader to run a winning race.

The bible tells us we are the light of the world. A city set on hill can't never be hidden. With this understanding, go out there and light up your world. Dominion is your birthright in Christ. God created everything and asked man to dominate over them all. What you think is what you will get. Your negativity will get you negativity, your positivity gives you a positive mindset.

WORDS OF WISDOM
- God is evolving you to strengthen you.
- If you trust God for a mansion, God can give you an estate.
- Love is not in the eyes; love is in the heart.
- If you stay with the word of God, you can stay informed forever.
- God is number one. Every other thing is number two.
- What you do not demand cannot be yours.
- God is a mighty ocean that does not run dry. You can fetch from him forever.
- Those who seek after darkness will never see the light of day.
- If you can dream it, you can see it.
- Faith means jumping from nothing to something. It also means leaving your Egypt to your Canaan land.
- Greatness in service.
- All hard work brings profit.
- Nothing will change until you start practicing change.
- If you fall, you can still stand up. It's only when you consider yourself a total failure that you remain on the floor.
- Lead the right people to the right place.

- Life is a process. You must submit to the processes too.
- If you are not a practical Christian, the devil will practically use you.
- If you don't study, you are dying mentally.

HOW DO I BRING MY DREAMS TO REALITY
- Pray and work hard. Don't accept defeat.
- Don't give up on dreams.
- Show kindness to others and help the poor.
- Go for knowledge.
- Study the word of God.

CHAPTER 9
PURPOSE PREVAILS
JO ANN LIPSCOMB

Philippians 1:5-7, says, "because of your partnership in the gospel from the first day until now, being confident of this, that he who began a good work in you will carry it on to completion until the day of Christ Jesus." (NIV) When you partner with God, He calls you to be His own and makes you aware of why you're here in the first place (your purpose). No matter what life tries to throw at you, no matter what disastrous plans Satan has for you, no matter what you think or others think, you can rest assured that God's purpose prevails. There are many times the knowledge of God had to get me through difficult times. I keep in mind that if it did not take my life, God has a lesson for me. If I'm still standing, God's purpose in my life is still standing and I can keep moving forward in confidence that my partnership with God is still intact. God's purpose in my life prevails.

Since the enemy has his eyes on me and throwing everything he can in my way to make me stumble, I must know what God has in his heart for me so I won't fall, give up, or live in a way that has no meaning. When you know that your life has meaning and significance, you begin to live life in a way that says, "I can truly do all things through Christ who strengthens me." Philippians 4:13 (NIV). You begin to live your life with confidence and whatever God's directives are in your life, your answer is always yes and amen.

When you know God's purpose prevails, all (heck) can fall down around you. But your thinking is, "If what has happened or what is happening didn't have the power to destroy me, then there must be a lesson God wants me to learn." When I take on this kind of mindset, that I'm not so quick to get offended and angry at God for not calming or stopping the storms immediately. I'm not so quick to throw my hands up and quit living for God because He didn't handle the problem like I wanted or thought He should have. I also do not so quickly blame others for something I should blame myself for due to bad choices or aliening myself with the wrong crowd. Even if this storm is my fault, I dare not count myself unworthy to continue being used by God.

Life has a way of making you feel like God is not able to handle the difficulties that come your way and somehow you get this notion that God needs help or you decide, "I will do it myself." Sadly, this is how many Christians backslide or turn completely from God back to the worldly living and never come back to the source that made heaven and earth. Scripture repeatedly shows us through the lives of others, that if God has a purpose for your life and He is in total control then His purpose will be accomplished and He will preserve and protect us from destruction.

The stories in the Bible are not for our amusement or a way to help us fall asleep; they are real and so are the people whose stories we are so fortunate to read about. These stories will strengthen, calm, encourage, rebuke, lead, protect, save and deliver, if you would just believe and allow God's word to saturate your mind, spirit and heart. You will began to learn by studying the scriptures that there is absolutely nothing too hard for God and that the same God you're reading about is the same yesterday, today and forever (Hebrews 13:8 NIV). If the purposes He started in others were completed, then that same God is ready, willing, and able to complete any and all works He has begun in you.

No Respecter of Person

God shows no partiality when it comes to using people for His purpose. Acts 10:34-35, says, "Then Peter began to speak: 'I now realize how true it is that God does not show favoritism but accepts from every nation the one who fears him and does what is right.'" (NIV) If you're telling yourself that you're not worthy to be used by God because of your past, or the predicament you're currently struggling with, know that this can't be further from the truth. As the saying goes, "Satan is a liar." God can and has used anyone He wanted to use whether you thought they were worthy or not. God ask permission to use anyone. So, if there's a calling on your life, stop doubting and trying to talk God out of using you like Moses tried. As you can see that didn't work because He chose us before anyone knew we existed! Thank God.

When God called me in that, "bedroom encounter", the first thing He said when I tried to resist Him was that He didn't stop by anyone's house to get their permission to use me. He had been waiting outside the doors of my heart. In other words, He was telling me that the decision to let Him into my heart and life was all mine, not anyone else. I even tried, like Moses, to recommend someone else I felt people would like, listen to and follow. But like Moses, He didn't listen to a thing I said, and continued to show me through visions and dreams what His purpose looked like. What a mighty God we serve, that even though He could accomplish His will on earth Himself, He chooses to use the same people who were so caught up in the sin He had to come to earth to die for. Makes you ask the question asked in Psalm 8:4, "What is mankind that you are mindful of them, human beings that you care for them?" (NIV)

This answer can be found in John 3:16, "For God so loved the world that he gave his one and only Son, that whoever believes in him shall not perish but have eternal life." (NIV) It is a love that gave and a love that keeps on giving no matter what we think about Him. There are no excuses you can give God as to why He shouldn't use you because according to 1 Peter 4:8, "Above all, love each other deeply, because love covers over a multitude of sins. So if you think you're too dirty, and your life has never been what others would have wanted for themselves, or like myself feeling unworthy due to being caught up in domestic and emotional abuse, think on these things."
Phillipians 4:8 - "And now, dear brothers and sisters, one final thing. Fix your thoughts on what is true, and honorable, and right, and pure, and lovely, and admirable. Think about things that are excellent and worthy of praise." In other words think, meditate and live on God's truth.

Can God Use Me in Spite of...
- Paul – Persecutor of Christians. On His way to Damascus was going to kill more Christians. But God had other plans for Paul.

- Peter – Impulsive, a liar, denied Christ, and used foul language. But God had plans for Peter and in one setting, after Christ died, over 3,000 men were saved from one message he gave.
- Moses – Murderer, had a speech impediment, and a coward. But God had BIG plans, He used Moses to deliver an entire nation from captivity.
- Esther – Jewish, exiled in Persia, young. But God had a plan for Esther; He used this young girl to find favor with a Persian king, became Queen in a foreign country and saved her nation from total annihilation.
- Hannah – Distraught, barren, ridiculed, and suffered from low self-esteem. But God had a plan for Hannah. She prayed for God to open her womb. He answered by giving her a son named Samuel, who became God's prophet, priest and judge in Israel.
- Lois and Eunice - Women, insignificant for their time, and poor. God had plans for those two women. They were Timothy's mother and grandmother who raised him to know God. Timothy went on to be discipled by Paul and led the church at Ephesus.
- Know that God is not confused; He knows exactly who you are and what your life has been or is all about. His purpose has the power to prevail over our mistakes, flaws and shortcomings. You are not a challenge for God and what He has planned for your life. We serve a God that can use everything about you as His personal platform to deliver, strengthen, heal, and save others who think they're

just as unworthy as you do. So, don't underestimate the power of God's calling on your life. He is all powerful, all knowing and everywhere at the same time, saving the ones who will accept Him as Lord and Savior and want to reign in eternity with Him.
- Put away all doubt regarding God using someone like you and be a part of God's master plan for your life and for others. Learn through studying the scriptures that if God can use these ordinary people to fulfill His purpose and will on this earth, than why would you not think He could use you to change the world one person at a time through the power of the Holy Spirit. You are who He had on His mind all your life! (Isaiah 63:3)

Prevails Over Circumstances

Everyone God used and still uses has something wrong with them. No one is perfect according to Romans 3:23 which says, "ALL have sinned and fall short of the glory of God," and Romans 5:8 which says, "But God demonstrates his own love for us in this: While we were still sinners, Christ died for us."(NIV) Some may have not done as much as others, but ALL are in need of a Savior and the only way to salvation and heaven is through our Lord and Savior Jesus Christ.

God's purpose prevailed over:
- The lion's den
- Death, the cross and the grave
- Barren wombs, addictions, anxiety and depression
- Domestic abuse, sexual abuse and abandonment

- Adam, the serpent and the fall
- Whatever is keeping you from being used by Him.

Know that the victory is already won!

If nothing mentioned above has or had the power to stop God's purpose, then why would you think anything you're going through or have gone through is powerful enough to stop the will of God in your life. There's nothing new you can come up with that will surprise God or make Him scratch His head according to Ecclesiastes 1:9 which says, "History merely repeats itself. It has all been done before. Nothing under the sun is truly new." (NLT) And nothing can hold you back, according to Isaiah 41:13 - "For I am the LORD your God who takes hold of your right hand and says to you, Do not fear; I will help you." (NIV) Even if the whole world is against you, Romans 8:31 says, "What, then, shall we say in response to these things? If God is for us, who can be against us?"

If God be for us, and our purpose comes directly from Him, and He is all-powerful, then why doubt and make excuses? Instead, surrender and let your response be what Mary's response was to Gabriel when approached with the will of God for her life. "I am the Lord's servant," Mary answered. "May your word to me be fulfilled." Then the angel left her," Luke 1:38 says. (NIV) She had no clue what Gabriel was talking about. All she knew was that his message came from God and if God was calling her to do something than she was willing to risk all, lose all and make her body available for God to accomplish His will for her life. Because she said, Yes, God sent His only son to atone for our sins and be the way to eternal life. Because God's purpose prevails, we're able to spend the rest of our lives in a place prepared just for us by God Himself. John 14:3 says, "And if I go and prepare a place for you, I will come again and receive you to Myself; that where I am, there you may be also." (NIV) Praise God!

Partnership

The day I accepted Christ was in my bedroom, while sitting on my bed feeling like all hope was lost in my life. I call this my, "bedroom encounter", God made it crystal clear that this union was a partnership and that I was not required to make His plans happen on my own. At first I wanted to ask Him if He knew I had raised two boys on my own with little or no help because I had to prove to the world and their father that I could do this parenting thing all by myself and that I had earned my supermom cape by being all things to all kids. So, to have God tell me that He needed my obedience not physical help was going to be a big challenge for the both of us, I could see it.

Playing tug-of-war with God is useless because He always wins. As I struggled with God, layers of myself began to fall off and more of Him began to take form. The more I tried to accomplish on my own, the more I became totally exhausted, asking God to take it back because I couldn't handle being in His lane. This partnership meant I had my lane, He had His and sometimes He would have mine too, but I would never be able to have His. It was confusing for me at first but as time went on everything He said began to make sense. In order for God to fulfill His will in my life, it would require 100% surrender. This is what is required of you in order to see the fullness of what God has in store. It will be difficult at first to give 100% over to God but believe me, when you start operating in your calling and Satan starts his attacks, you will thank God over and over again for, "taking the wheel," in your life. John 10:10 says, "The thief comes only to steal and kill and destroy; I have come that they may have life, and have it to the full. (NLT)

Yes, God's purpose will and does prevail over any and all things, but you must stay connected by drawing close to Him so when Satan comes to attack, and he will, his attacks will be to no avail. James 4:7 says, "Submit yourselves, then, to God. Resist the devil, and he will flee from you." (NIV) Know that you serve and have agreed to partner with God who is so powerful that according to James 2:19, "You say you have faith, for you believe that there is one God. Good for you! Even the demons believe this, and they tremble in terror." (NTL) and that in the end according to Philippians 2:10, "that at the name of Jesus every knee should bow, in heaven and on earth and under the earth."

With this knowledge and understanding of who you are and to whom you belong, you should never be doubtful, afraid, timid, reluctant, tempted or easily persuaded to go against any directives God gives. Instead, you should, "Therefore, my dear brothers and sisters, stand firm. Let nothing move you. Always give yourselves fully to the work of the Lord, because you know that your labor in the Lord is not in vain." 1 Corinthians 15:58 (NIV) Nobody likes working for absolutely nothing. Know that when you work for the Lord you have everything to gain and absolutely nothing to lose.

In Conclusion: You Become Who You Serve
- Philippians 2:5, "Let this mind be in you, which was also in Christ Jesus." (NIV) Study and meditate on the word of God as often as you can so when you find yourselves in difficult situations God can convict your heart, give you the word to say or lead you away. Whatever is on the mind and heart of God is on yours.
- Psalm 37:23, "The LORD directs the steps of the godly. He delights in every detail of their lives." (NLT) No matter what direction you're going if you allow God to lead. Know that you're heading in the right direction. It doesn't matter how many twists and turns you have to make. He could lead you to be light in dark places or light on a hill.
- Psalm 119:11, "I have hidden your word in my heart that I might not sin against you." In order for you to feel the things God feels, your heart has to stay protected, hiding His word there. When you are touched by the things of the world, you have a tendency to develop a hard heart that is easily offended, will abruptly attack and become emotionless. To prevent these things, you must allow God's word to saturate and touch your heart.

This world can be a scary roller-coaster ride that can and will have a negative effect on the heart if you aren't allowing God's word to be its protector and shield. When you partner with Christ, He becomes your thoughts, what you meditate on day and night, your actions and director of your steps. He becomes your all and all in everything you do and according to Psalm 46:1 - "God is our refuge and strength, a very present help in trouble." (NIV)

You truly become who you serve. Be careful to avoid conforming to the ways of the world, be mindful of the company you keep, be wise with who you allow to counsel you and speak into your life and be cautious of how deceptive Satan can be through people's slick motives. Yes, God's purpose prevails but we must be wise in the decisions we make regarding how we live our lives. Know that Jesus is your wonderful counselor. Isaiah 9:6b says, "And he will be called Wonderful Counselor, Mighty God, Everlasting Father, Prince of Peace." (NIV) For this reason it's up to Him to choose who will give you guidance. Amen.

CHAPTER 10
PURPOSED TO TAKE ACTION, DESPITE OF AND REGARDLESS TO
DR. ONIKA L. SHIRLEY

As a woman of purpose, I've got more than a little interest in mindset. I have discovered on my journey that mindset is what ultimately determined my attitude and my strategic approach to the innumerable amount of challenges I have faced in this lifetime. In my purposeful life, my unstoppable mindset has been carefully erected from early childhood. In the days of my youth, I watched and I listened to the things that were being done and the things that were being said by my mother, my stepfather and others adults around me and I created a belief system around work, work ethics, and what was supposed to be "normal". We must realize that sometimes our personal beliefs and our planted "normal" may work completely against our purpose and best interest. I learned that there's hope because our mindset is changeable. The right mindset will not only change and direct your life, but it can influence the lives of those you're called to serve. Our mindset can bring great success or complete failure. I had to decide to accept the rules of truth. I accepted the absolutes: water is wet, fire is hot, air is needed to breathe and live but beyond these simple truths I had to ask a few questions. Why was I created? Who was I meant to be? Who was I created to serve? I discovered that I am a woman of purpose and I am UNSTOPPABLE.

UNSTOPPABLE women must be positioned to be heard and not just seen. When we position ourselves to be in the right place, in the right state of mind, and guided by the principles of God we can be great. This is not the position of greatness for self-seeking pleasures, but for the God honoring positioning that will enable us to be great for others and to build the kingdom of God. When we are positioned for greatness and we are walking in our purpose, we find a certain fulfillment that closes gaps in our souls. After being in two life changing accidents I thought to myself that life was still worth living. Neither of these accidents were fender benders. The results were more than minor. I can hardly explain the excruciating pain I experienced. I knocked out my front tooth, broke another one in half which had nerve damage, lost the femur bone out of my left thigh, injured my left knee, broke my left ankle, broke my left jaw, and broke the same three toes in both accidents and not to mention the scars to the skin. The road to recovery and restoration was long. It was going to take a lot of hard work and determination to be restored. I knew I would need to work hard to recover and I did, but it all started in my mind. The doctors told me there were certain activities that I would never do again and some activities would take a long time to start performing again, but I challenged myself one day at a time. I thought I would become mobile one movement, one activity, and one step at a time.

I was only nineteen years old when I had these car accidents. This was during the prime of my life. I was a senior in high school. I had no friends to visit me while I was in the hospital and some days I felt like I was all alone just lying there waiting to get out of the hospital. My family was there for a while, but they had to go back to work and I understood that because no money was being made sitting at the hospital with me. It seemed like everything I was working for had been stripped away, but

God. He never allowed me to sit in pity. He never allowed me to sit back and feel sorry for myself. God gave me the strength, the wisdom and the desire to keep moving. Romans 5:3 says, "Not only so, but we also glory in our suffering, because we know that suffering produces perseverance." During this time, I was able to lean on the Word of God. I was able to manage all that had happened to me during this devastating time because of God's amazing grace. During this time, I found that I really was UNSTOPPABLE and I knew that I was saved from death to serve.

Despite the odds against me and despite what the doctors told me, I persevered. God helped me to pick up the broken pieces, mend the broken bones, adapt to my current situation, and start putting my life back together again. During this time, my finances were not looking good. I had a three-year-old daughter, a house and of course bills. I was a hard worker and all the work I did was for the wellbeing of my daughter and me. I went from working and going to school, to not working and not going to school wondering how to travel the fastest way down this road of recovery. I was in the hospital for almost a month and a half. I learned to manage. I laid there with hope, hope of getting out, hope of going back to school, and hope to work again. I had hope and I knew one day everything was going to be all right. After being discharged from the hospital, the road of recovery had to begin. I could hardly do anything for myself. I was immobile for a while on my own. I couldn't go to the bathroom by myself, I couldn't get up, and I couldn't wash myself without assistance. I was truly at the mercy of others. My mother, my grandmother, my sister and my niece helped me out a lot. I honestly wouldn't have been able to make it without them. I had to use different machines, breathing devices, a hospital bed at home, and baby monitors to function on a daily basis. Physical therapy was initially expected every day an hour and fifteen minutes away from home. I couldn't do that because I wasn't able to drive and I didn't have a driver every day so I transferred my therapy to my hometown and that was a mistake. I walked on crutches for an entire year until one day I said I don't care if I walk with a limp. I am not doing this any longer because the crutches were causing so much pain under my arms. I sent them out to the storage building and I fought. I fought to walk, I fought to maintain my balance, and I fought to be mobile because I was determined. I was UNSTOPPABLE and a growing woman with a purpose for God. I was courageous and bold.

At the beginning of my journey to recovery, my income was zero. I went from working one to two jobs and a lot of overtime to nothing. I had to choose not to pay credit card bills and forsake my credit in order to pay household necessities like rent, light, water, gas and food. I had to get on welfare and food stamps for a short period of time until my SSI benefits (Supplemental Security Income disability) were approved. I was disabled. I could no longer do what I once was able to do at this young age. I thought to myself that I know that God didn't create me for this, and I know he doesn't want me to live like this the rest of my life. I was too young to live waiting on a check every

3rd of the month. I went on a job hunt and challenged my disability. I got a job as a housekeeper at Fitzgerald's Casino. I worked, I cried, and I endured daily swelling and pain, but my purpose was much greater than my pain. I told myself I would have to toughen up and deal with it and overtime it would get better. I had to get strategic. I needed to know that all things were possible with Christ. After work every day, I had to go home and soak in alcohol and Epsom salt to prepare for the next day. Once I made up in my mind that I was not going to use my injury as an excuse to sit at home drawing $568 a month, I called the Social Security Administration and told them I was working and they can cut my check off. I have worked for the last 19 years and I went back to school to fulfill my childhood dream that was delayed due to my car accidents for four years. Although the start of college was delayed from high school graduation to the 1st day I actually step foot in the class, I went. I enrolled because I was determined, and I was UNSTOPPABLE. I went to school for 10 years straight nonstop without a break or even a thought to take a break. I received my Associates in Education, Accounting and Finance Certificate, Bachelors in Business Accounting and a Master's in Business Administration. The entire time I was enrolled in school, I worked and raised my children as a single mother.

My life was being restored and my faith and my drive were stronger than ever. I continued to persevere and just when I thought my life was getting better it got worse. I was terminated from my job, one that I had worked very hard on and was told that in a couple days I would be promoted to a lead auditor. Instead of being promoted, I was terminated. I never questioned the act of it all because God had a plan for me. I had been praying for an opportunity to be off on Sunday and at this particular job Sundays were very difficult to get for off days so God removed me from that job to see if I was serious about my request. I wanted to attend church and now I am a faithful servant at my local church and I have been ever since I lost that job 12 years ago. After losing that job, I picked up extra days at the school because I was already subbing on my off days from the casino so I was well known and wanted. I also worked at McDonalds which was very difficult for my leg because of the concrete but I pressed until something better came along. I landed a job in manufacturing as a quality inspector and in one month the favor of God was on my life. In one month, I went from an hourly position to a salary position where I was off on Saturdays and Sundays. I have held seven positions within the company where I now hold the position of Customer Service. The plant closed six months before writing this book, but God showed me favor. My employment at this company had been rewarding although sometimes challenging.

My life has been well acquainted with suffering, but I am destined to serve those God have entrusted to me. God has a work for me to do and He has something for you to do, too. I conquered the strongholds of my past which helped me to birth Action Speaks Volume. It was a very slow process because I didn't know where to start and I allowed my environment to be an initial excuse until I stopped thinking from my own backyard. I had to reach out and get help because I didn't have everything I needed, but I was determined to get it. I am UNSTOPPABLE. I am determined to help women and little girls break the strongholds on their minds, build unshakable confidence, and live a life of purpose. I don't want to see others allow their past to hinder them and to hold them back like my past did for a period of time in my life. A lot of times I simply wouldn't deal with them. I packed them up and put them away as if they never happened, but this is not good because it comes back to haunt you in a midlife crisis. I kept secrets of anger buried in my heart. I was ashamed, I was angry, and I was horrified. I decided to no longer allow my past to continue to delay my purpose so I decided to make a real change. My change had to be bigger than a great idea. I had to make the change in my head, my reality. I got busy and I really focused on what needed to be done. I first had to identify the areas in my life that needed a change, I identified how the change would interface with my ongoing life and then I created the structure of my change by strategically planning what needed to happen. God kept me through it all. He knew the plans He had for me and my life. He knew he could use me for His glory and that's why I was tested. He told me that's why I went through the storms and that's why I had to go through some things because I wouldn't be a good witness without the experience. We can't teach people that in which we have not learned. I am walking in purpose and my trials and tribulations qualified me to inspire, to motivate and to encourage other women to press through the obstacles of life. I didn't allow adversity, the odds against me, setbacks, obstacles, disappointments, nor being overlooked to stop me because I am UNSTOPPABLE and my PURPOSE is being REVEALED.

I won't allow "NO"thing and "NO"body stop me from doing what God has called me to do. I was raised without a father and I turned out okay. My mother didn't have a high school education, but she made sure I got one and she did go back to school to get her high school education and now I have four degrees. I was sexually assaulted at the age of 10, but I've found peace with my aggressor. I was in two life changing car accidents, but I am still here. I lost the first home I attempted to buy through foreclosure. I was blessed to buy another one and it was paid for several years before the one I lost would've been paid off. I was a teenage mother and she turned out to be a beautiful young lady. She graduated from UCA of Conway, AR, with her Bachelor's degree in Health Education in 2016 and she is an amazing mother to my granddaughter Baby Aubrey and my baby girl is in her second year at UCA, trying to find her purpose in this life. I am UNSTOPPABLE and I knew I had to keep moving for my girls as well as for myself. I also have twin boys that require me to keep moving. I must be a great example for all my children but their individual purposes will be discovered by themselves. There's a call on my life to serve. I found my purpose by reaching out to others as a mentor, a coach, a substitute teacher, an instructor, a supervisor, a manager, a parent, a foster parent and an adoptive parent. In 2018, I graduated with my Doctorate Degree in Christian Counseling so now I am also serving in my purpose as a counselor.

My purpose is the reason in which I exist. I am a servant. I have a heart to help those who are hurting, suffering, in pain, struggling with past hurts and disappointments. I recognized my purpose early in life because I knew what made me cry and I knew what hurt my heart. I started to really walk in my purpose when I became a foster parent in 2008 and then became an adoptive mother in 2011. I simply listened to my hurts, my heart and my tears. I want to please God and I am confident and certain in conquering life and business because I have the word of God to propel me to the next level. God will help me help the women I am called to help. I will encourage her to look at herself from within. She should examine her feelings in certain environments and examine her thoughts in the mist of certain circumstances. Be bold and be confident while always being ready to serve. Being in a position of purpose requires you to post up and act as if though you are the only one able to get the task done.

When you are purposed to take action, you will become UNSTOPPPABLE despite of and regardless to the prevailing circumstances. You are UNSTOPPABLE! You are UNMOVABLE! You are an ACTION TAKER and you are called for a PURPOSE.

Purpose to Take Action, Despite of and Regardless To!
Interactive questions

Do you know why you were created? Do you know your divine purpose? Do you know who you were created to serve?

Action Takers Challenge: I challenge you to be determined to feel empowered. You must remember life will happen, but purpose can be discovered and walked in despite of and regardless to what happens in your life.

Question 1
What one thing keeps you up at night for hours at a time, every time you think about it?
Think about that **ONE** thing that makes you cry and you know deep in your heart something should be done about. You have decided to take action no matter what. You have made up your mind that you're going to take action even if you must do it by yourself.
Think about it and write it down.

Question 2
What makes you feel determined and energetic?
We all have that feeling from something. This is the thing or person that you don't mind getting up for and you don't mind spending money on it. What is it that makes you feel like you are **UNSTOPPABLE** despite of the odds and regardless to the situation and opposition?
Think about it and write it down.

Question 3
What task makes you lose track of time?
Reminisce on those activities where you were so involved that your dinner time has passed you by. Think about the time where you said "time has just flown by" or "where did the time go?"
Write it down.

Question 4
What is the one thing that keeps coming back to haunt you because you are running and ignoring it?
You have tried running from it. You have tried to ignore it. You have avoided talking about it. What does God want you to do? You know what God has told you, but you have told yourself that's not what you want to do. What is it? Build your relationship with God, ask for forgiveness, and make His will your first priority. God will never bring you to something He is not going to bring you through.
Write it down.

Question 5
What has God put in your heart to do?
Think about the thoughts you have had to help. You must realize that they are not just random thoughts. Be quiet and still and listen to the voice of God.
Write it down. Listen to your heart and to the voice of God.

Question 6
What makes you sad and what makes you cry?
We all have things that make us sad and make us cry. When you are in that position, are you able to keep going?

Do you strive to take action? Do you just sit and wait? Write it down.
We were all created for a reason. We can't allow the ups and downs of life to stop us. Stop being a free prisoner of your past experiences and build your life in the NOW.

Question 7
How can you position yourself to be unstoppable? List 5 things you can do in the next 30 days.
1.
2.
3.
4.
5.

Meditate on the following scripture (Proverbs 16:9)
"In their hearts humans plan their course, but the Lord establishes their steps." Proverbs 16:9

Sister, you're UNSTOPPABLE. God is going to make sure his word will not return unto him void or twisted. There's no "thing" and no "body" that can stand up to God's power, purpose, plan, and glory.
Write it down.

How has God moved in your life? Have you gone back to say thank you?
Read over the UNSTOPPABLE word for 21 days (Repeat when necessary)

U-Uncover your purpose and stop hiding
N-Nurture your God-gifted purpose
S-Specialize in your purpose
T-Track your impact
O-Operate in purpose and on purpose
P-Perfect your calling and continue to improve
P-Prioritize God's will and God's way
A-Authorize God to use you. He is not going to force you
B-Believe you are unstoppable, keep it moving
L-Listen to the voice of God
E-Eliminate ALL excuses

Three (3) Activities you can do you that show you are an unstoppable woman
1. Write down your own set of unstoppable behaviors?
2. Host/attend events that will intensify your purpose.
3. Pray and Mediate daily

UNSTOPPABLE "Think about it" exercise (meditate and answer the following questions)

- How prepared were you for the tragedies in your life?

- What makes you an unstoppable woman?

- What tragedies have you gone through in life that you overcame?

- What nuggets did you used to overcome your tragedies that could help somebody else?

- Although your course was changed, did you continue to move forward?

Exercise:

Every time you're knocked down and faced with tragedy, document how long it takes you to get up. Really think about it and write it down.

Three proven strategies I implemented to create an impactful transformational change.

1. I believed that God was and is bigger than anything I could've ever faced. When I was faced with obstacles, disappointments, and the tragedies of my life, I talked to God. I established a relationship with my Heavenly Father and I started to pray. I prayed and I prayed and I prayed again.

2. I remained true to myself. I discovered that I was unstoppable when I followed the whispers of God and I found my authentic self.

3. I transformed my life by changing the images in my head that were downloaded and taken by someone else. I had a positive attitude and I wrote and spoke my own "I AM" statements. I started standing in the mirror looking the person on the other side eye to eye and spoke life into her. I spoke encouragement to her and I allowed her to be the person she was created to be through the words I spoke to myself.

Take a look at my "I AM" statement to give you an idea of how to write your own. I challenge you to write your own "I AM" statement. This is not to be arrogant nor prideful. Tell yourself things you want to hear and the things you want to see and believe in your life.

I AM a woman of God. I AM an overcomer. I AM a survivor of sexual abuse. I AM grateful for every trial and tribulation of my life because they were learning experiences I AM happy, healthy, and wealthy. I AM a fighter. I AM not a quitter. I AM a go getter. I AM worthy. I AM enough. I AM not affected by the opinions of others. I AM beautiful. I AM smart. I AM a woman of my word. I AM confident.

You were created for a purpose so walk in your purpose on purpose and declare that you are truly UNSTOPPABLE.

CONCLUSION
DR. ONIKA L. SHIRLEY

As I thought about my final remarks for this book, Ephesians 1:11 came to mind. In Christ, we are chosen for God's glory. That makes us glorious and it gives a significant meaning and purpose in our lives. We have talked about serving God, discovering our purpose, embracing our purpose, being fruitful and multiplying and so much more. We know that deep inside every person God created a hunger to live a life of significance and purpose. God has entrusted humanity with certain resources, gifts, talents, and abilities. All these attributes rightfully belong to God. Our sole responsibility is to live by that trust by managing what he has given to us individually according to his design and desire. God reveals through his word his desires for our lives then equips us to live it out to the fullest through his Holy Spirit, who empowers, restores, comforts, and reforms us by grace.

"In him we were also chosen, having been predestined according to the plan of him who works out everything in conformity with the purpose of his will." Ephesians 1:11 NIV

I pray that you were blessed and your purpose was revealed while reading the words within the pages of this God-breathed book. They can be impactful and life changing. I hope you took the time to read through it slowly and carefully. Meditate on the scriptures and wait for God to speak to your heart. Allow Him to show you why you are here and to whom you were created to serve. Live your life on purpose, be intentional, and serve all that you can. God will not allow you to fail if what you are doing is His will. Honor God by serving him and by serving his people. YOUR PURPOSE HAS BEEN REVEALED!!!!

www.ingramcontent.com/pod-product-compliance
Lightning Source LLC
Chambersburg PA
CBHW050653160426
43194CB00010B/1926